Motivational Tips

Romana Hoque

pencil

ISBN 978-93-5667-095-2
© Romana Hoque 2022
Published in India 2022 by Pencil

A brand of

One Point Six Technologies Pvt. Ltd.
123, Building J2, Shram Seva Premises,
Wadala Truck Terminal, Wadala (E)
Mumbai 400037, Maharashtra, INDIA
E connect@thepencilapp.com
W www.thepencilapp.com

DISCLAIMER: *The opinions expressed in this book are those of the authors and do not purport to reflect the views of the Publisher.*

Author biography

Romana Hoque is motivational speaker and author. She mainly work on create awarness about depression and Islimc motivation.

She already published four books which are available on amazon.com.

He academic field is law but she devoted herself to Islamic reasarch.

CONTENTS

Motivation 1

Life is not always beautiful, but it is always precious, so, do not let it to waste. It doesn't matter how many time your life let you down. Turn back and fight back, never give up.

Motivation 2

Forgive and move on. Do not give second chance who let you down.

Motivation 3

You cannot make happy everyone, so, stop try to be make happy everyone.

Motivation 4

Less expectation less pain. Always remember human has limitation. Only expect from your Lord Almighty.

Motivation 5

Try hard till your last breath, who knows may be success is waiting at the very end of your life. Never lose hope.

Motivation 6

Success can be start from your back yard garden. It is not always necessary every action need to be grand and appreciate in this world. Your simple and small deeds collectively can bring your success.

Motivation 7

High ambition is not evil what is wrong it is greed. If you failed to check your greed , it will destroy you every possible way you hardly can imagine. So, work hard to control your greed. It does not matter how much educated you are greed will make you ignorant.

Motivation 8

Never underestimate yourself and do not wait for others appreciation or judgement.

Chapter 9

Do not be boastful and arrogant. Arrogancy is ugly and annoying.

Motivation 10

Be truthful. Avoid falsehood, it has negative
impact on personality.

Motivation 11

Do not judge anyone. Judging other person is a sin.

Motivation 12

Outer beauty does not define bauty, it is manner and humblenes define someone beauty.

Motivation 13

If you want to be just,first apply justice in your home.

Motivation 14

Knowledge itself will not make you intellect.
It is wisdom which will make you intellect.

Motivation 15

How childish it is when any one say it is mine. We are a traveller for short period of time. All these things we assume we possess it is given to us for a short period of time to make comfort our journey. We possess nothing.

Motivation 16

Always keep good thoughts about your Almighty Creator. Never despaired from His Mercy.

Motivation 18

Knowledge is infinite, never be proud and over confident about your knowledge.

Motivation 19

Never try for short cut. If foundation is not enough strong it will be collapsed.

Motivation 20

Be modest and decent these beautify your personality.

Motivation 21

What is wrong it is wrong even entire society or globe say it is right still it is wrong.

27

Motivation 22

No one is 100% perfect. Do not expect perfections from any one. Only Allaah the Almighty is Perfect.

Motivation 23

Learn to accept positive criticism but stay away from fault-finder. Your critics will help you to grow but fault-finders will destroy your confidence.

Motivation 24

Always seek for beneficial knowledge .

Motivation 25

Be stick with your goal one day success will kiss your feet.

Motivation 26

Some blessings are test and some sufferings are reward. So, never boastful with your blessings and never judge any one based on their hardship.

Motivation 27

Name, fame, power and money are material success which are temporary. Ultimate success depends on piety and earn mercy from Almighty.

33

Motivation 28

Do not look at others sins, concentrate on own sins.

Motivation 29

Leave those matter which are not bothering you.

Motivation 30

You can leave your legacy two ways, through your offspring and through your beneficial work.

Motivation 31

Knowledge remove the ignorance and ignorance is a mother of every evil.

Motivation 32

Not every knowledge is beneficial, only seek for beneficial knowledge.

Motivation 33

Death is not a end of your journey it is begining of another journey.

Motivation 34

Do not tolerate opression.

Motivation 35

Do not choose extreme path always choose middle path.

Motivation 36

Always remeber ingratitude is a sickeness of heart. Do not be ingratitude.

Motivation 37

Envy is something which consume person himself/herself who effected by envy. Stay away from envy.

43

Motivation 38

Love yourself but do not be selfish and self-centric person.

Motivation 39

If you cannot do any good for others at least
don't do any harm to others.

Motivation 40

Do not be fatalistic, do your best and rest leave to Almighty. Whatever the result come accept the decree of the Almighty.

Surely, He is the best planner.

Motivation 41

Always remember this life is short and temporary, so, the suffering of this life is also temprary.

47

Motivation 42

Do not let the material world consume you.

Motivation 43

Arrogance is the dark personality, so, stay
away from it.

Motivation 44

Becareful when you will select a friend.

Motivation 45

Never neglect others. Always remeber all the blessings we get all belongs to the Almighty Allaah.

Motivation 46

Indecency is filthy and has negative effect on personality.

Motivation 47

Respecting others ideology and thoughts doesnot means you have to follow those views or ideologies.

Motivation 48

Set a goal what you can achieve.

Motivation 49

Socialize with better people.

Motivation 50

Money and power can give you temprary respect, it is your wisdom can bring you ever lasting respect.

Motivation 17

Be authentic does not mean be wild. Its mean be who you are and avoid show off. Its doesn't mean you have to break every social norm just because its goes against your desire and ideology.